Skye Terrier

Old English
Sheepdog

Wire-haired Terrier

oston Terrier

Dandie Dinmont

Beagle

Bedlington Terrier

riffon
xellois

Cocker Spaniel

Pomeranian

Basset Hound

Schipperke

Boxer

Dogs that haven't been trained are a nuisance to themselves, their owners and the neighbours, but a well trained dog is a happy dog that you will be proud to own. Your dog is affectionate and eager to please you – with patience and perseverance, following the guidelines in this book, you can train it properly to take its place in the family circle. As ex-Chief Inspector Jack Howell MBE, internationally acknowledged expert on police dog handling, said, "A dog is as good as its owner. Make sure that you have a good dog."

Acknowledgments
Cover photograph is by Tim Clark. The photographs on pages 6, 7, 8, 9 (top) and 10 are by courtesy of the Natural History Photographic Agency. The illustration on page 12 is by Keith Logan.

Training your Dog

by WYNTER WESTON

photographs by JOHN MOYES
and TIM CLARK

illustrations by KATHIE LAYFIELD

Ladybird Books Loughborough

THINK TWICE – AND THINK AGAIN!

Whether it's a goldfish or a Great Dane, a tabby kitten or a tortoise, if you buy a pet of any kind, you are assuming a responsibility for a living thing which must not be taken lightly.

And of these pets, a dog is both the most demanding – in terms of effort, time and expense – and probably the most rewarding in terms of companionship.

So if you've decided you would like a dog, make absolutely sure you can say yes to these questions:

1 Have you, or someone in the family, enough time to spend with it and on it? It needs attention every day of the week, every week of the year – it needs regular exercise, grooming, and of course feeding. *It is in fact someone's full time job.*

2 Can you afford to keep it? A grown dog needs a surprising amount of the right kind of food – and both meat and prepared dog foods have become expensive.

3 Have you got a suitable place for it to live? If it is going to live outside, it must have a comfortable, secure place where it will not be a nuisance to others.

4 Have you a friend who will look after it when the household is on holiday? If not, this means boarding kennels – which again are expensive.

5 Finally, how much do you know about teaching your dog to be obedient? And are you prepared to try to learn to train it? *A well trained dog is usually a happy dog.*

Which kind of dog?

WHICH KIND OF DOG?

If you are confident you have the right answers to all the questions, you must now decide whether to have a puppy or an adult dog.

Generally speaking, it is best to have a puppy, because, although adult dogs will often fit in well and make good companions, a puppy will become a member of your household more quickly and easily.

A dog as big as this Pyrenean Mountain Dog needs much more space, exercise and food than a smaller dog would require

What kind of dog do you want: small, medium or large? Much will depend upon where you live. A flat will

obviously not be suitable
for a large dog. In fact,
flats are not really suitable
places in which to keep
dogs at all. (Unless, of
course, they have very easy
access to the ground floor,
where the animal can
relieve itself without
offending other people.
Dogs fouling public places
are a great annoyance and
often contravene local bye-
laws.)

The size of the dog is usually important. Most people
consider that a small dog fits into the average household
better and needs less exercise, and there is a wide choice:
terriers, miniature poodles, beagles, Shetland sheepdogs,
and so on.

West Highland White Terrier

The question of the dog's coat has to be considered.
Long haired dogs, although often elegant, require
considerable attention if they are to be clean and well
groomed. Short haired or wire haired dogs may be easier
to manage. Also some dogs may require clipping or
stripping in warm weather, which is quite an expensive
business. Another point to consider is that some children
and adults, especially if asthmatic, react badly to long
haired dogs.

Dalmatian – Dogs like setters, Dalmatians and Labradors need a lot of exercise

However, there is another very important factor which is often overlooked. It is the question of temperament, and what may be called 'train-ability'. As a general rule, terrier breeds, which often appear to 'fit the bill' as far as size is concerned, are less easy to train than Labradors which are somewhat larger. There are, of course, exceptions to every rule and certainly all sizes of poodles – toy, miniature and standard – can be extremely obedient. It is fair to say however that some of the medium-size breeds are easier to train than many smaller breeds.

Yorkshire Terrier

White Poodle

It is not essential to have a pedigree dog — many cross-breeds and mongrels make very obedient and good companions. Dog or bitch? This is a personal matter. Some people consider that dogs are less trouble. This is because when bitches are in season — every six months — it is necessary to restrict them for three weeks to make sure that they do not have access to a dog. It is said that bitches are more faithful than dogs but there is no evidence to prove this.

Mongrel puppy

Looking after your puppy

LOOKING AFTER YOUR PUPPY

It is always advisable to obtain your puppy, whatever its breed, from a reputable source. By doing so you will have a much better chance of getting a healthy, well developed, well grown puppy, free from the many hereditary and infectious diseases to which puppies are prone. Puppies are ready to leave the litter at about eight weeks old. By this time they are quite capable of feeding upon a diet of milk, fresh meat, cereal, vegetables, gravy etc, and should be fed four small meals a day.

Do not leave partly eaten food to be contaminated by flies and dust or your puppy will become ill. Keep the water bowl and food dish clean at all times and never feed him scraps that have been left lying about.

Do not let anyone feed the puppy from the meal table or it will come to expect this and will be a nuisance. Let it learn that its food is always in one place, in its own dish, and that it is not fed anywhere else.

One of the first things you will want to do is to give your puppy a name so that it will come to your call. This is a personal matter, but your puppy will find it easier to learn a short name, preferably of one syllable. Dogs do not really understand every word that is said to them, and it is much better to keep your words short and simple.

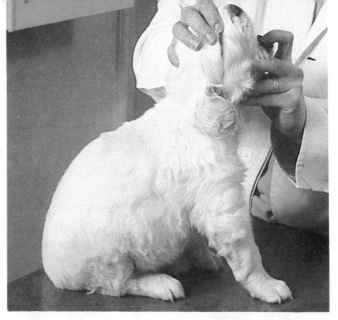

At this stage your puppy requires regular food and plenty of sleep; this is the secret of healthy growth. This can be impeded if the puppy is troubled by round worms. Your local veterinary surgeon will prescribe tablets and tell you at what age they should be given. In addition, at from eight to twelve weeks old, it will be necessary to have the puppy vaccinated. The vet will usually recommend a vaccine which will give immunisation against Distemper, Infectious Hepatitis and Leptospirosis and he will administer the vaccine by injection, in two doses with a fortnight's interval between the doses. For ten days to a fortnight after its vaccination, your puppy should be kept away from other dogs – preferably at home. 'Booster' vaccinations are needed from time to time, and your vet will tell you when they should be given. These vaccinations are vitally important if your dog is to remain fit and healthy.

From the age of eight weeks to six months, your puppy will be growing rapidly. Its life will be spent in eating, sleeping and playing. Meanwhile you should be observing it very carefully to find out all you can about its personality.

Your puppy needs affection, but remember that puppies' habits are those of small animals. Kissing and fondling them can prove very unhealthy.

House and social training

HOUSE AND SOCIAL TRAINING

A puppy's habits are formed in the early months, and it's the owner's job to see that those habits are good ones. During this period you can lay the foundations for a well behaved and happy dog, but it takes patience and consistent treatment.

First of all, a puppy has to be clean in the house and in order that it can achieve this, it must be let outside at frequent intervals. If — and this happens sometimes in the early days — your puppy wets or makes a mess inside, be patient. It will learn by habit and will soon associate the act of being let out, with relieving itself.

Inside, the puppy needs somewhere of its own: a box or basket in a corner where it can sleep. It should quickly claim this as its own and appreciate it as a haven of peace and security — which is important to the puppy.

It needs to feel wanted, too. Affection is necessary, but it should be tempered with common sense. Your puppy should be taught that furniture is for humans, and that climbing over chairs and settees will be firmly discouraged. All members of the household have to help with this good-habit forming. Insist on a certain pattern of behaviour, and make sure that others in the house insist on the same rules. There must always be consistency in dealing with your dog, otherwise the animal will be confused and will not know how to respond.

The house training months can become a crucial period in the life of a puppy. For one thing, it very often becomes the sole responsibility of the mother of the house when the family are out during the day (at work or at school), and she has already plenty of work to do. It is essential, therefore, to work out a good routine right from the start, so that the job is made as easy as possible.

A place of its own

A PLACE OF ITS OWN

Hundreds of dogs are turned out of their homes every year, unwanted, to roam the streets and countryside. Many of them are taken by the police, and others finish up in RSPCA kennels. Of these, some are reclaimed, some find new homes, and the remainder are humanely destroyed. If dog owners would realise that a dog needs a place of its own (even if it is the house dog) fewer dogs would be turned out in this way. Every dog needs a place where it can be away from the house at times during the day when it may be inconvenient for the household to have it inside.

It is not too difficult to make a run outside where your dog, although restricted, can be quite content and at the same time be safe and unable to get into mischief. The run does not need to be a great size. A minimum size might be 2½ by 1½ metres, constructed of posts and strong gauge wire, with a height of 1½ – 2 metres. Concrete slabs are convenient for the floor, enabling it to be swilled down.

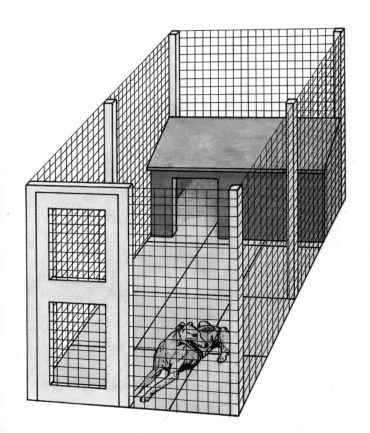

A small wooden kennel inside the run provides the dog with shelter from the elements. Clean water should always be available. A large beef shin bone will occupy the puppy and help to prevent it from becoming bored.

In a run of this kind, the dog, particularly now that it is growing up, can have a change of scenery and interest − which is good for both animal and owner. Equally important, the owner knows exactly where his dog is and ensures that it is not being a nuisance to neighbours and the public in general.

This arrangement, when the dog becomes used to it, will contribute to a harmonious and happy relationship between dog and family.

Introducing cars and collars

INTRODUCING CARS AND COLLARS

By this time you have probably bought your puppy a
collar and lead complete with a name tag. This should
give the dog's name, the owner's name, and the address.
Although your puppy should never be loose on the road,
it might escape or run away when frightened, and its
finder will want to know where to return it to. It is a
good idea to accustom the young animal to a collar and
lead. However, it is a mistake to take your puppy with
you everywhere you go. In the first place, this practice
gives a young puppy too much exercise. Secondly, if you
wait until the puppy is more mature and you can teach it
to walk by your side quietly, it is less likely to develop
such bad habits as tugging you along, or jumping up at
every passer-by.

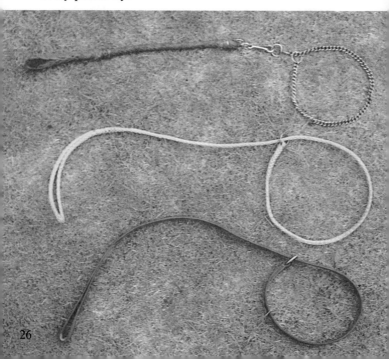

THE WRONG WAY

When putting on
a choke chain or
a lead, the chain
must run from your
hand, over the dog's
neck and then under
its jaw – never
the other way
round, or the
chain will not
loosen when the
dog stops pulling

THE RIGHT WAY

Along with house and social training must go the day-to-day education of the young dog, of which travelling is an important part. Most dogs enjoy riding in cars, but the owner should consider it carefully beforehand.

Dogs should learn immediately which is their place when riding in a car. You should bear in mind that your dog may leave hairs on the seat or climb in with wet, muddy feet. To help you and your dog, it may be advisable to cover the dog's 'seat' with an old rug, blanket or sheet.

Puppies are at first frightened of entering cars and much can be done to encourage confidence. Put your puppy in the car for a few minutes, stroke it, and talk to it in a soothing fashion.

You can, too, offer it a biscuit whilst inside, so that it may associate the car with some pleasant experience. A few minutes daily will soon give the puppy confidence and it will not be long before it will enter voluntarily. The first journeys should be short ones, gradually lengthening as the puppy becomes more confident.

Here again, just as with house training, the dog should be encouraged from the start to occupy a certain position in the car and to stay there. It must learn that the car is not a place to play in, since disastrous consequences may follow if it distracts the driver in any way. A dog should be discouraged (very firmly) from riding on the seat at the front of the car, and also from putting its head out of the window when travelling. It must always be put on the lead before leaving the car.

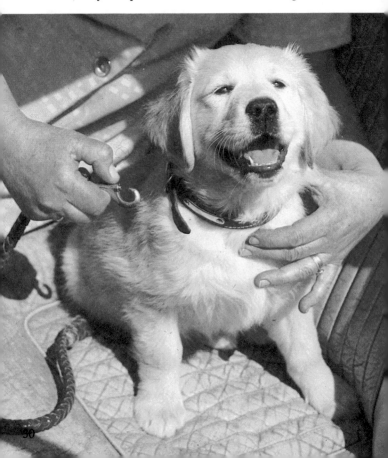

Basic obedience training

BASIC OBEDIENCE TRAINING

So far, you have been trying to guide your puppy's behaviour along the right lines. The next step is to decide when you are going to begin some definite plan of training. This training is often known as 'hand' training, or, perhaps more correctly, basic training. Initially, this training must be continuous, which means that once the lessons are started, they must be practised regularly.

Six months of age can be considered to be a reasonable time to start some serious work, although some puppies may not be ready until they are nearer nine months. You will have to judge for yourself by the way the puppy responds.

Your training should take place where there are no distractions, either to the dog or to yourself. A field would be ideal, but a back garden will do equally well. In fact a backyard with a bit of room can be just as satisfactory. The three main ingredients for success are patience, concentration and consistency.

Walking to heel on the lead

The first lesson is to teach your dog to walk to heel. The dog must walk on your left side, so that its right shoulder is as close to your left knee as possible. It must not be allowed to pull in front or to one side, or to lag behind. It is advisable when teaching walking to heel, to use a 'choke' chain (one with big links) or a slip lead of leather or cord, which are more effective for training purposes than a collar and lead. It is most important to place the chain or lead on the dog in the correct manner, so that it will slacken off when the pressure is released. (See page 27)

33

The lead is now placed on the dog and the handler gives the command HEEL and walks off at a fairly brisk pace, with the lead held in a slack position. If the dog pulls and tries to get in front, it must be firmly brought back by a jerk of the lead and a firm command of HEEL. Should the dog pull to the side, the same procedure should be carried out, but immediately the dog returns to the correct position, the lead must be slackened.

Most dogs tend to pull persistently in front and they must be brought back to the correct heel position by a

sharp jerk of the lead, upwards and backwards. It is useless to pull against the dog's shoulders. The jerk should always be made upwards and backwards.

Some dogs will lag behind, or even lie down. If this happens the handler should give a jerk on the lead with the command HEEL and should encourage the animal by tone of voice. Nothing is gained by dragging the dog along – it is pointless and cruel.

Often it is a good idea to hold the lead in the right hand, across the body, leaving the left hand free to encourage the dog, by slapping the thigh and repeating the command HEEL encouragingly. Sometimes an object like a piece of cloth, carried in the free hand, will attract a reluctant dog's attention and encourage it to walk on. A biscuit in the hand, in this situation, will often act as a successful bribe. Once the desired result has been achieved, bribery must be discontinued.

As soon as the dog comes into the correct heel position, it should be praised to give further confidence and encouragement. Do *not* grab at your dog. Make a series

of right and left turns. Do *not* attempt heel work by always walking in a straight line. Where the dog is persistently trying to pull forward, the handler should constantly turn about. In so doing, the dog is then left in the correct position or a little behind.

The length of these early lessons must be short – certainly not more than ten minutes. Young dogs quickly become bored and tired and the handler's patience may be frayed. Praise the dog when it has done well, but only praise good work.

Sitting on command

Walking to heel should be practised for ten minutes each day, and this will soon show progress. Varying your walking pace will help to keep the dog alert, and you should try to make the training an enjoyable time for the animal. While you are training it to walk to heel, the dog should also be taught to sit on command. When it comes to a halt, give the command SIT, at the same time firmly pressing down gently on the rear end of the dog with the left hand and lifting the dog's head with the lead. Hold this position for a few seconds, then release the dog and give the command HEEL as you walk on. Each time the command SIT is given the dog should be pressed down immediately and the duration in the sitting position should be lengthened a little each time. The important thing to remember is that when the puppy is given the command SIT it *must not move* until given a command to do so. *Never allow your dog to get up without a command.* If it does move, it must be returned to its original sitting position *immediately.*

These early lessons in Heeling and Sitting must be repeated exactly at every lesson. Constant repetition of the lesson is essential, care being taken by the handler to be consistent with his or her commands and the way they are given, and to correct faults constantly. The aim should be perfection. If the dog sits sideways by the handler, or too far forward, or to the rear, the handler must stoop down and gently but firmly correct the position.

Walking free at heel

If quiet progress is being made, the dog will begin to walk obediently to heel and sit on command. The lead by this time should be quite slack and the dog should be hardly aware of it. When the handler is satisfied that this lesson is satisfactory, the dog can now be allowed to walk at heel without the lead. Place the dog in the sitting position and remove the lead with as little fuss as possible. Give the dog the command HEEL and move forward, encouraging the dog by patting the thigh with the left hand. If the lead work has been done thoroughly, the dog will walk in the correct position. If the dog shows signs of moving away at the side, or going too far in front, it must be given a firm command HEEL and encouraged to return to the correct position. If, however, the dog is constantly breaking from the correct position, the lead should be replaced and walking to heel on the lead resumed. When the free at heel lesson is attempted again, instead of removing the lead, loop it round the dog's neck, and then proceed with the free at heel lesson. If this proves successful, it should be repeated a number of times and then the lead removed, as before. Initially make each lesson of short duration. The important thing is to avoid discouraging the dog by trying to grab it if it moves from the correct position. Patience is the key, and encouragement and praise when the dog does well.

Sitting to a stamped foot

Running parallel with the heel free exercise should be an extension of the SIT exercise. Coupled with the spoken command SIT, the dog should learn to go down in the sitting position at the stamp of a foot. It is a simple matter to give a little stamp each time the vocal command is given. The dog will soon learn to associate the foot signal with the sitting position.

Sitting to a long blast on whistle

It is an added refinement to teach your dog to sit at a blast from a whistle. This can be taught at the same time as the verbal command SIT and the

stamped foot. All that is necessary is to give a long blast on a whistle, then give the verbal command. This long blast should be blown every time the dog sits. The dog will quickly associate the whistle with the action and will eventually sit on each óccasion.

The type of whistle used does not really matter – a loud one is not necessary. If you are able to whistle, the dog will learn to accept that signal equally well, providing it is used frequently.

Sitting at a distance

Now it is time to teach the dog to remain sitting when the handler leaves it. The exercise should be done carefully, step by step. Place the dog in the sitting position. Move to about half to three-quarters of a metre in front of it, at the same time raising one hand with the palm showing to the dog (similar position to a policeman's stop signal). If the dog shows signs of rising repeat the command SIT firmly. Remain in the position for a minute or two, then return to the side of the dog. Each time the lesson is repeated, the handler moves progressively farther away from the dog.

To have success with this important exercise, three things must always be remembered:

1   *Do not continually repeat an exercise in any one period of training.* Success in two attempts should be sufficient. Wait until next training to repeat and occasionally leave it out altogether.

2   If the dog moves forward, even very slightly, the handler must go to it *and return it exactly to the original sitting position.*

3   The hand signal must always be the same. At no time must the dog be allowed to deviate from the command without correction – but do not forget to praise it, when it has done well.

With careful and patient training, it will be possible for the handler to leave the dog in the sitting position and walk away thirty or forty metres, or even out of sight. However, a good handler will always concentrate on the dog and never take anything for granted. Never accept a standard less than excellent, and remember always to correct errors immediately. By this time the dog should be able to walk to heel without the lead and remain steady when left in the sitting position, at all times.

Recall from a distance

This needs to be introduced very carefully, otherwise the good habits you have already taught may be upset. So far, when the dog has been left in the sitting position, the handler has always gone back to collect it, and nothing has been said about recalling the dog when it is at a distance from the handler.

In order to call the dog up, the handler calls the dog by name, gives the command HEEL, blows a series of short blasts on the whistle, and at the same time pats the thigh as added encouragement. When the dog joins the handler it should take up the correct sitting position by him or her until commanded to do otherwise. It is most important that calling up the dog from the sitting position does not happen too frequently. If you do it too often, the dog will come to anticipate that it will happen

every time it is left in the sitting position and will tend to move towards you before commanded to do so. This is a bad habit, which is often more easily acquired than cured. If you make a practice of going up to your dog and praising it for remaining where it was commanded, and calling it up only occasionally, you are much more likely to achieve a lasting result.

WHAT SHOULD NOW HAVE BEEN ACHIEVED

If the handler has carried out the training programme carefully and correctly, it should be possible to achieve the following:

The dog should walk to heel, off the lead, quietly and obediently. It should sit on command and remain so whilst the handler walks on, then returns, walks past the dog and beyond it. The handler then returns to the dog and 'picks it up' (gives it an order to get up and walk on). It should be possible to repeat this on numerous occasions, the handler always obtaining complete obedience from the dog.

The handler should be able to give the dog the command SIT and then walk away out of sight and remain so for a minimum time of sixty seconds. (The time the dog is left sitting must be built up to, gradually and carefully.) The dog must remain sitting until the handler returns and gives it the command to move.

49

IMPORTANT POINTS TO REMEMBER

1   Do not let the length of the training session drag on too long. Fifteen minutes well spent, with the dog enjoying it, is worth much more than half an hour, when the dog may become bored and inattentive.

2   If you try to make each training session interesting and enjoyable, you are more likely to get response. Always try to end on a happy note.

3   During training, the handler must concentrate exclusively on the job. There should be no distractions for dog or handler. If you are mentally tired or have other matters on your mind, postpone the session.

4   Be definite and insist that everything that you do in training is done correctly. Do not settle for 'near enough', or your dog will develop a sloppy standard.

5   Do not use a lot of words of command. SIT, HEEL, NO (given firmly, when the dog must desist instantly), together with the dog's name, will be enough to get through the basic training. The upraised hand will emphasise that the dog must remain sitting and should always be used clearly. The whistle and stamped foot commands are very desirable refinements.

6   Try to remain patient with the dog. A handler can easily get frustrated with a dog which does not readily respond to repeated commands. Return the dog to its kennel and try another time.

7   The key to success is patience and repetition, and the ability to concentrate upon and understand the dog which is being trained.

"A dog is as good as its owner. Make sure that YOU have a good dog."

Ex-Chief Inspector Jack Howell MBE

Index